thirty-something-ye ar-old

Kristine Duran

BookLeaf Publishing

India | USA | UK

Presentation by *BookLeaf Publishing*

Web: www.bookleafpub.com

E-mail: info@bookleafpub.com

ISBN: 9789363316645

First edition 2024

For Princess Pumps

Late Night Reflections

I'm in my zone, no calls tonight,
Silence speaks, the city's quiet.
Midnight thoughts, they keep me tight,
In this moment, I'm my own riot.

Can't escape the shadows cast,
Memories linger, but they won't last.
Rise and grind, my pace is fast,
Still, I cherish what's in the past.

Eyes wide open, dreams unfold,
The hustle's hard, the nights are cold.
Every story left untold,
In the silence, I find my gold.

Don't disturb my peace, my way,
I need this solitude to stay.
In the darkness, I find my day,
Navigating through the gray.

Battles fought and wars within,
Through the losses, I find my win.
Quiet nights, they start to spin,
In this chaos, I'm born again.

Echoes of the past, they fade,
New paths taken, old ones laid.
In my silence, strength displayed,
In this quiet, I'm unafraid.

So let the world keep spinning wild,
In my silence, I'm reconciled.
No disruptions, undenied,
In this moment, I'm revived.

On My Grind

I'm back on my grind, no looking behind,
Stacking my wins, can't waste any time.
Pushing the limits, I'm crossing the lines,
Focused on mine, gotta shine like a sign.

Hustle's relentless, I'm in it to win,
No slowing down, no need for a friend.
Building my empire from start to the end,
Moves that I make, they don't need to defend.

Talk all you want, I'm deaf to the noise,
Focused on paper, no time for the toys.
Making these plays, I'm one of the boys,
Riding the wave, my life's full of joys.

Heat in my veins, the fire's alive,
Hungry for more, I'm ready to thrive.
Cutting the ties, I had to survive,
Now it's my moment, I'm ready to drive.

Scheming on ways to multiply stacks,
Money and power, no turning back.
Living my truth, no need to act,
Everything earned, no need to subtract.

Rising above, they watching me fly,
Doubt in their eyes, but I'm touching the sky.
Focused and driven, my limits defy,
On my BS, ain't no telling a lie.

Victory's near, I feel it inside,
Nothing to fear, no reason to hide.
On my own path, no one to guide,
Making my mark, it's one hell of a ride.

Electric Pulse

Through the night, neon lights,
Chasing dreams, city sights.
Heartbeats echo, beats align,
Lost in rhythm, feel the shine.

Electric pulse, it guides my way,
Lost in music, night and day.
Every step, a journey grand,
In this beat, I understand.

Broken hearts and shattered dreams,
In this life, nothing's as it seems.
Picking pieces, finding grace,
In the rhythm, find my place.

Voices whisper, shadows play,
Through the dark, I find my way.
Music's magic, heals the soul,
In its arms, I feel whole.

Glitter tears, falling down,
Through the pain, I'll wear my crown.
Every note, a story told,
In this journey, I am bold.

Lost in sound, I'm found again,
Through the highs, through the pain.
In this beat, I see the light,
Through the darkness, I take flight.

Electric love, it fuels my heart,
In this world, I'm set apart.
Through the chaos, through the noise,
In this pulse, I find my voice.

Late Night Call

Late night, my phone lights up again,
Your name on the screen, it feels like then.
Back to the times, we'd talk till dawn,
Now it's a ghost, those days are gone.

You used to call me on my phone,
In the twilight, not alone.
Now it's echoes in my mind,
Searching for what we left behind.

I see your pictures, living your life,
No more calls, no late night strife.
Used to be the one you'd ring,
Now I'm just a forgotten thing.

Changed your style, you're moving fast,
Left me standing in the past.
Used to know you, every line,
Now it's like you drew a sign.

I miss the days we'd talk so free,
Now it's just a memory.
All the times we used to sing,
Faded with that hotline bling.

But I'm moving, finding me,
In the space where I can be.
Late night calls, they fade away,
Looking forward to a brighter day.

Still, sometimes, when the night is long,
I think about where we went wrong.
But life moves on, and so will I,
Beneath the stars, an open sky.

City Nights

5 AM, the city's asleep,
My thoughts are heavy, running deep.
Streetlights flicker, shadows dance,
Lost in the rhythm, caught in a trance.

Winter's cold, but my mind's ablaze,
Memories blend in a foggy haze.
Whispers of nights, love and regret,
Scenes I play, can't forget.

Messages left, unread, unseen,
Fragments of moments, what might've been.
Heartbeats echo, through the dark,
Tracing the lines of every spark.

Roaming these streets, where we used to meet,
Lonely paths beneath my feet.
Skyline glows, your face appears,
Through the silence, I hear your fears.

Times have changed, but I'm still here,
Haunted by whispers in the atmosphere.
You moved on, found your peace,
Yet in my heart, you never cease.

City nights, a melancholic tune,
Reflections dance beneath the moon.
In the quiet, I find my way,
Through the shadows, the break of day.

Dreams of past, they intertwine,
In the city's pulse, I find the sign.
Though you're gone, the memories stay,
In this freestyle, I find my way.

Midnight Confession

Late nights, shadows on the wall,
Heartbeats echo, do you feel the call?
Thoughts of you, they twist and turn,
In the darkness, I still yearn.

Have you ever felt the pull?
This tension, it's unbreakable.
Questions linger, answers hide,
Do I dare to let it slide?

Whispers in the midnight air,
Memories of times we shared.
Every glance, every touch,
Do I wanna know if it's too much?

Cigarette smoke and neon lights,
Wandering through endless nights.
Can you hear the silent plea?
Do you feel the same for me?

Dreams of you, they haunt my sleep,
Secrets buried, buried deep.
Should I ask or let it lie?
Do I really wanna try?

Tangled in this web of doubt,
Can't seem to find a way out.
In your eyes, what do I see?
Do I wanna know if you're with me?

Echoes of your voice remain,
Lingering like a sweet refrain.
Every moment, every sign,
Do I wanna know if you're still mine?

Torn between the fear and hope,
Hanging by this fragile rope.
In the end, what will I find?
Do I wanna know what's on your mind?

Silence speaks, but words betray,
Caught in this game we play.
In the shadows, truth will show,
Do I really wanna know?

Move, Move

Turn up the lights, the night begins,
Heartbeat pounding, under our skins.
Sweat and thrill, we're feeling alive,
In the chaos, we thrive.

Bassline hits, we're in the groove,
Every step, we move, move.
Eyes lock, the room starts to spin,
Lost in the rhythm, where do I begin?

Neon lights, a fever dream,
Pulse of the night, we're the main theme.
Hands in the air, bodies collide,
In this frenzy, we can't hide.

Dancing through the midnight fire,
Fueled by heat, driven by desire.
Echoes of laughter, a wild chase,
In this moment, we find our place.

Shadows twist and lights ignite,
In this dance, we own the night.
Spinning fast, no time to lose,
In the rhythm, we choose.

Hearts racing, we don't slow down,
Every beat, we own this town.
In the dark, we shine so bright,
Dancing rebels, taking flight.

Lost in the music, lost in the sound,
In this whirlwind, we're unbound.
Move, move, till the break of day,
In this dance, we find our way.

No tomorrow, just tonight,
In this dance, everything feels right.
With every beat, with every sway,
In the music, we'll stay.

Cold Nights

In the night, so cold, so heartless,
Lost in a city that's dark and ruthless.
Neon lights, they cast a glow,
On a love that's come and gone, slow.

You said you'd be there, now you're gone,
Left me stranded, all alone.
Echoes of your words, they haunt,
Promises you made, they taunt.

Empty streets, I walk alone,
Searching for a place called home.
Heartbeats cold, frozen tight,
In the shadows of the night.

Tears that fall, they turn to ice,
Memories, a high-priced vice.
Love was once our guiding star,
Now I wonder where you are.

You were my warmth, now you're frost,
In this game, I feel the cost.
Heartless actions, no remorse,
Left me drifting off course.

Time moves on, but scars remain,
In the silence, I feel the pain.
Cold as winter, your touch was warm,
Now I'm lost in this storm.

Faces pass, but none are you,
Searching for a love that's true.
In the night, I find my way,
Through the heartless games we play.

Enduring Love

Through the storms and endless rain,
We walk the path of joy and pain.
Love so fierce, it won't let go,
Through the highs and the low.

Eyes that shine, through tears and smiles,
We've journeyed on for countless miles.
Holding tight, despite the fight,
Guided by a stubborn light.

When the darkness cloaks the day,
And words like arrows, cause dismay,
We find the strength to carry on,
In the heart where love is drawn.

Bruised and battered, hearts entwined,
Love remains, both cruel and kind.
Through the scars and the strife,
It's the pulse that gives us life.

Even when we lose our way,
And the world is cold and gray,
Love's a fire that won't subside,
Burning fierce, deep inside.

Hands that hold through every storm,
Keeping each other safe and warm.
Though we bend, we do not break,
Love endures for its own sake.

Through the nights so dark and long,
In our hearts, a steadfast song.
Stubborn love, a guiding star,
Leading us no matter how far.

With every tear, with every fight,
We find our way back to the light.
For in this love, we see the truth,
Stubborn hearts, forever youth.

Wrecking Ball

You came in like a storm so fierce and wild,
A force that tore down walls I thought secure.
With every glance, with every touch, I smiled,
Yet in your wake, I found no lasting cure.

I built my walls so high, so strong, so sure,
Believing they would keep my heart at bay.
But you broke through with fire and allure,
And turned my night into a brightened day.
Each word you spoke, a thunderclap of sound,
Each kiss, a lightning strike upon my soul.
You shattered me, left pieces on the ground,
A heart in ruins, struggling to be whole.

You came in like a wrecking ball of love,
Now I am left to heal and rise above.

Vampire

You sank your teeth into my trusting heart,
A charming smile, a touch so cold and sly.
I fell for you, entangled from the start,
Unveiling truths beneath the midnight sky.

Your words were sweet, a honey-coated lie,
Deceptions masked in love's deceitful art.
You drained my light, left me a ghostly sigh,
A shadow of the girl who played her part.
The nights we shared, they feel like distant
dreams,
A haunting dance beneath the pale moonlight.
You stole my breath, unraveling at the seams,
A vampire feasting on my fading light.

Now I reclaim the strength you tried to take,
A heart revived, no longer yours to break.

Horror Binge

In the still of midnight, where shadows weave,
She revels in whispers that chill the air.
A girl enchanted by the thrill of fear,
Wrapped in horror's embrace, she finds her flair.

The screen flickers with a ghostly luminescence,
Monsters' growls and screams shatter the
silence.
Her eyes sparkle with eager anticipation,
Drawn to haunted tales, bold and unafraid.
From ethereal phantoms to the undead's
mournful wail,
She revels in each frightful, chilling scene.
In the depths of darkness, where echoes linger,
She is enraptured by the mysteries unseen.

In the realm where nightmares bloom and thrive,
She discovers a thrill that keeps her spirit alive.

Are your riding?

Late nights, city lights, I'm caught in a trance,
Scrolling through my phone, waiting for a
chance.
Thinking 'bout you, girl, can't get you off my
mind,
Wondering if you feel the same, or if I'm just
blind.

Do you love me? Are you riding?
In my feelings, no denying.
I need to know, are you down for the ride,
Or just a shadow, slipping out with the tide?

Memories of us, replay on repeat,
Our laughs, our fights, the times so sweet.
You've got me lost, in a maze of thoughts,
Heartbeats quicken, tangled in knots.

Text bubbles popping, but no reply,
Leaves me hanging, staring at the sky.
In my zone, all alone, thoughts of you,
Wondering if your feelings are true.

I'm here waiting, hoping you'll see,
In this game of love, it's you and me.
Do you love me? Are you riding?
In my feelings, no more hiding.

Don't Speak

Whispered words that used to soothe,
Now linger in the air, bittersweet and smooth.
Once our voices harmonized,
Now silence echoes where love once thrived.

Eyes that held secrets, now turn away,
In the twilight of love, we drift and sway.
Every touch, once a promise deep,
Now a memory in the silent keep.

Don't speak, for words will only break,
The fragile peace we try to fake.
Unspoken truths hang in the air,
A heavy burden, too much to bear.

We used to dance in the light of the moon,
Now shadows creep, our hearts attune.
Silence grows, a chasm wide,
Love's whispers lost, like the ebbing tide.

Don't speak, your eyes tell all,
In the quiet, we watch our love fall.
Unraveling threads, a delicate weave,
In the silence, we both grieve.

Let's hold onto the ghosts of our smiles,
In the quiet, we'll walk our separate miles.
For in the silence, love's truth we seek,
Don't speak, my heart's already weak.

I miss you

In the quiet of the night, shadows creep,
Memories of you, haunting my sleep.
A whisper in the dark, a ghostly sigh,
I miss you more with every breath I cry.

Your voice, a distant echo in the void,
Our laughter now a silence, once enjoyed.
In the stillness, I hear your name,
A hollow ache, an endless flame.

In the darkened room, I feel your touch,
A phantom kiss that hurts too much.
The emptiness you left behind,
A constant presence in my mind.

I miss you, like the moon misses the sun,
In the twilight, where our dreams were spun.
A love that faded, like a dying star,
Leaving scars that never heal, no matter how far.

In the stillness, I replay our song,
Every note, where we belonged.
But now the melody is a broken tune,
A heart that aches beneath the moon.

I miss you, with a longing deep,
In the shadows, where our secrets keep.
In every whisper, in every sigh,
I miss you, and wonder why.

In the Stillness of Night

In the quiet of the night, when the world hushes its bustling symphony, I find myself drifting into memories of you. It's like a gentle breeze carrying fragments of our moments together, whispering softly in my ears. I miss you, not just with my heart but with every fiber of my being.

There's a certain emptiness that lingers in the air, a void that only your presence could fill. I find myself tracing the outlines of your absence, like a sculptor shaping a sculpture that will never be complete. The memories we shared, they are etched into the walls of my mind, each one a precious gem that I hold onto tightly.

Sometimes, in the stillness of the night, I can almost hear your laughter echoing in the distance. It's like a melody that plays on repeat, a bittersweet reminder of what once was. And I find solace in those fleeting moments, as if you're here with me, if only for a breath.

But then reality sets in, and I'm reminded of the silence that now surrounds me. It's like a deafening roar, drowning out the echoes of our past. I miss you, like a sailor lost at sea, yearning for the familiar shores of your love.

In the darkness, I search for traces of you, a glimmer of hope that maybe, just maybe, you'll come back to me. But deep down, I know that some things are meant to remain in the realm of memories. And so, I hold onto them, like fragile glass, cherishing every shard of our love that remains.

Summer Breeze

The summer night arrives like a gentle whisper, carrying with it the fragrance of blooming flowers and the melody of chirping crickets. The windows are open, inviting the cool evening breeze to dance through the room, rustling the curtains in a playful embrace.

Outside, the sky is adorned with a tapestry of stars, each one a tiny beacon of light in the vast expanse of darkness. The moon, a radiant pearl, casts a soft glow over everything it touches, painting the world in hues of silver and shadow.

The air is alive with sounds of summer: the distant laughter of children playing, the rhythmic chirping of cicadas, and the occasional rustle of leaves as a gentle wind sweeps through the trees. It's a symphony of nature, a harmonious blend of sights and sounds that lull the senses into a state of peaceful tranquility.

Inside, the ambiance is cozy and inviting. The soft glow of lamplight illuminates the room, casting warm shadows that flicker and dance along the walls. The scent of freshly cut grass

mingles with the sweet aroma of jasmine,
creating an intoxicating perfume that fills the air.

I sit by the open window, a gentle breeze
caressing my skin, and I lose myself in the
beauty of the night. Time seems to stand still as I
watch the stars twinkle overhead, each one a
silent wish waiting to be whispered into the
universe.

In moments like these, the world feels magical,
as if anything is possible. It's a lovely night,
filled with the promise of dreams and the quiet
serenity of summer's embrace. And as I close my
eyes and breathe in the sweet summer air, I
know that this moment will linger in my heart
long after the night fades into dawn.

Thuggin it out

In the concrete jungle, where dreams collide,
We thug it out, with hearts open wide.
Life's battles, we face them head-on,
In the struggle, we find strength to carry on.

From the streets to the corners we roam,
Thuggin it out, making this place our own.
No handouts, just hustle and grind,
In the game of life, we leave our mark behind.

Through the trials and tribulations we endure,
Thuggin it out, with hearts pure.
We may stumble, we may fall,
But we rise again, standing tall.

In the midst of chaos, we find our rhythm,
Thuggin it out, with unwavering determination.
No fear in our eyes, just fire in our soul,
In the face of adversity, we take control.

So here's to thuggin it out, day by day,
In the struggle, we find our own way.
With resilience and courage, we pave our route,
Thuggin it out, no doubt, no dispute.

Unrequited

High above the clouds, I soar,
In a metal bird, longing for more.
The world below, a distant sight,
As I chase dreams in the endless flight.

Unrequited love, like gravity's pull,
Keeps me grounded, a heart so full.
But up here, among the stars so bright,
I find solace in the endless night.

The engine hums a soothing tune,
As I gaze at the moon, lost in the swoon.
Thoughts of you, a bittersweet pain,
A love unreturned, like drops of rain.

But as the plane glides through the sky,
I let go of the tears I've cried.
For in this moment, I'm free to be,
A heart in flight, soaring, wild and free.

So let the winds carry me away,
From the love that couldn't stay.
I'll embrace the sky, my endless love,
A flight of fancy, high above.

Writing Poetry

Writing poetry is like diving into a vast ocean of emotions, thoughts, and dreams. It's a journey where words become brushstrokes, painting vivid landscapes of the soul. Each poem is a story waiting to be told, a melody waiting to be sung.

There's a certain magic in the process, a dance between inspiration and imagination. It starts with a spark, a fleeting idea that ignites a flame within. From there, words flow like a river, meandering through valleys of feelings and climbing peaks of expression.

Sometimes, it's a whisper in the wind, a soft murmur that grows into a symphony of verses. Other times, it's a thunderstorm, a torrent of words crashing against the page, demanding to be heard.

Writing poetry is a catharsis, a release of pent-up emotions and hidden truths. It's a way to make sense of the chaos within, to find beauty in the mundane, and to capture fleeting moments of bliss or sorrow.

Each line is a brushstroke on the canvas of existence, creating patterns of meaning and depth. It's a delicate balance of structure and spontaneity, of rhythm and rhyme, weaving together a tapestry of imagery and symbolism.

In the end, writing poetry is about connection. It's about reaching out across time and space, touching hearts and minds with words that resonate. It's a gift, a legacy, a testament to the human experience and the power of language to transcend barriers and unite souls.

Rain

Upon the rooftops, rain begins its dance,
A gentle rhythm on the window pane.
Each drop a note, in nature's song's expanse,
A symphony of life, a soothing bane.

The sky in tears, it sheds its heavy load,
As clouds release their burden to the earth.
The air is cleansed, a purity bestowed,
In every drop, a tale of death and birth.

The trees sway gently, leaves drink in the rain,
A dance of gratitude, a timeless waltz.
The earth receives the gift, a fertile gain,
A quenching drink for nature's thirsty salts.

So let the raindrops fall, a soothing balm,
A melody of life, a healing calm.

www.ingramcontent.com/pod-product-compliance
Lightning Source LLC
LaVergne TN
LVHW010946200726

843509LV00013B/2300